In loving memory of Mum and Dad
and of Bev

The words of Ecclesiastes 3:1-8
are taken from the King James Version of the Bible.

This edition published in 2006 under license from
Frances Lincoln Limited by Eerdmans Books for Young Readers
An Imprint of Wm. B. Eerdmans Publishing Company
255 Jefferson SE, Grand Rapids, MI 49503
PO Box 163, Cambridge CB3 9PU U.K.

Library of Congress Cataloging-in-Publication Data
Bible. O.T. Ecclesiastes III, 1-8. English. Authorized. 2006.
To everything there is a season / [illustrated by] Jude Daly.— 1st ed.
p. cm.
ISBN 0-8028-5286-6 (alk. paper)
1. Bible. O.T. Ecclesiastes III, 1-8—Criticism, interpretation, etc. 2. Bible. O.T. Ecclesiastes III, 1-8--Pictorial works. I. Daly, Jude. II. Title.
BS1473.A88 2006
223'.8052034—dc22
2005012676

06 07 08 09 10 6 5 4 3 2 1

Set in Providence
Printed in China

To Everything There Is a Season

JUDE DALY

EERDMANS BOOKS FOR YOUNG READERS

To everything there is a season,

and a time to every purpose under the heaven:

A time to be born,

and a time to die;

A time to plant,

and a time to pluck up that which is planted;

A time to kill,
and a time to heal;

A time to break down,
and a time to build up;

A time to weep,

and a time to laugh;

A time to mourn,

and a time to dance;

A time to cast away stones,
and a time to gather stones together;

A time to embrace,
and a time to refrain from embracing;

A time to get,

and a time to lose;

A time to keep,
and a time to cast away;

A time to rend,
and a time to sew;

A time to keep silence,

and a time to speak;

A time to love,

and a time to hate;

A time of war,

and a time of peace.

To everything there is a season,

and a time to every purpose under the heaven.

To everything there is a season,
and a time to every purpose under the heaven:
A time to be born, and a time to die;
A time to plant, and a time to pluck up that which is planted;
A time to kill, and a time to heal;
A time to break down, and a time to build up;
A time to weep, and a time to laugh;
A time to mourn, and a time to dance;
A time to cast away stones, and a time to gather stones together;
A time to embrace, and a time to refrain from embracing;
A time to get, and a time to lose;
A time to keep, and a time to cast away;
A time to rend, and a time to sew;
A time to keep silence, and a time to speak;
A time to love, and a time to hate;
A time of war, and a time of peace.

Ecclesiastes 3:1-8